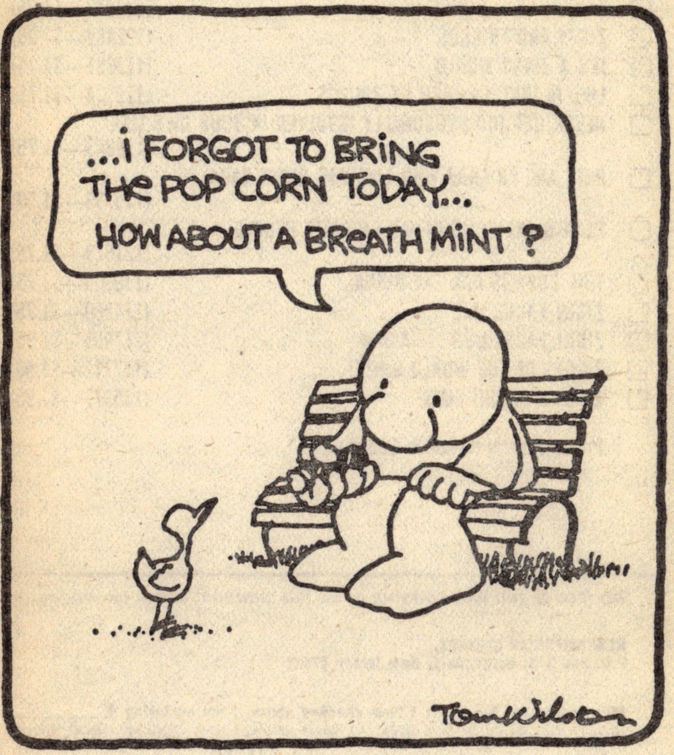

More Humor by Tom Wilson From SIGNET

		(0451)
☐	ZIGGY WEIGHS IN	(131754—$1.95)
☐	ZIGGY'S SHIP COMES IN	(128842—$1.95)
☐	ZIGGY AND FRIENDS	(122488—$1.95)
☐	IT'S A ZIGGY WORLD	(119681—$1.75)
☐	LIFE IS JUST A BUNCH OF ZIGGY'S	(119924—$1.75)
☐	NEVER GET TOO PERSONALLY INVOLVED IN YOUR OWN LIFE	(119843—$1.75)
☐	PETS ARE FRIENDS WHO LIKE YOU RIGHT BACK	(115783—$1.50)
☐	PLANTS ARE SOME OF MY FAVORITE PEOPLE	(121619—$1.75)
☐	THIS BOOK IS FOR THE BIRDS	(119606—$1.75)
☐	ZIGGY FACES LIFE	(114280—$1.75)
☐	ZIGGY FACES LIFE ... AGAIN	(117905—$1.95)
☐	ZIGGYS OF THE WORLD UNITE!	(112717—$1.50)
☐	ZIGGY'S IN AND OUTS	(135377—$1.95)

Prices slightly higher in Canada

Buy them at your local bookstore or use this convenient coupon for ordering.

NEW AMERICAN LIBRARY,
P.O. Box 999, Bergenfield, New Jersey 07621

Please send me the books I have checked above. I am enclosing $_____
(please add $1.00 to this order to cover postage and handling). Send check or money order—no cash or C.O.D.'s. Prices and numbers are subject to change without notice.

Name_____

Address_____

City_____ State_____ Zip Code_____

Allow 4-6 weeks for delivery.
This offer is subject to withdrawal without notice.

ZIGGY'S HIGH HOPES

by Tom Wilson

A SIGNET BOOK
NEW AMERICAN LIBRARY

NAL BOOKS ARE AVAILABLE AT QUANTITY DISCOUNTS WHEN USED TO
PROMOTE PRODUCTS OR SERVICES. FOR INFORMATION PLEASE WRITE
TO PREMIUM MARKETING DIVISION, NEW AMERICAN LIBRARY,
1633 BROADWAY, NEW YORK, NEW YORK 10019.

Copyright © 1984 by Universal Press Syndicate

All rights reserved. No part of this book may be used or reproduced
in any manner whatsoever without written permission except in the
case of reprints in the context of reviews. For information write
Andrews, McMeel & Parker Inc., a Universal Press Syndicate
Company, 4400 Johnson Drive, Fairway, Kansas 66205.

Published by arrangement with Andrews, McMeel & Parker Inc., a
Universal Press Syndicate Company

ZIGGY® is syndicated internationally by Universal Press Syndicate

This Signet edition of *Ziggy®'s High Hopes* comprises the second
half of *Ziggy®'s Big Little Book 2: Alphabet Soup Isn't Supposed to
Make Sense!*, originally published by Andrews, McMeel & Parker
Inc. *Ziggy®'s Ins and Outs*, available in a Signet edition, comprises
the first half.

SIGNET TRADEMARK REG. U.S. PAT. OFF. AND FOREIGN COUNTRIES
REGISTERED TRADEMARK—MARCA REGISTRADA
HECHO EN CHICAGO, U.S.A.

SIGNET, SIGNET CLASSIC, MENTOR, PLUME, MERIDIAN AND NAL
BOOKS are published by New American Library,
1633 Broadway, New York, New York 10019

First Printing, October, 1985

1 2 3 4 5 6 7 8 9

PRINTED IN THE UNITED STATES OF AMERICA

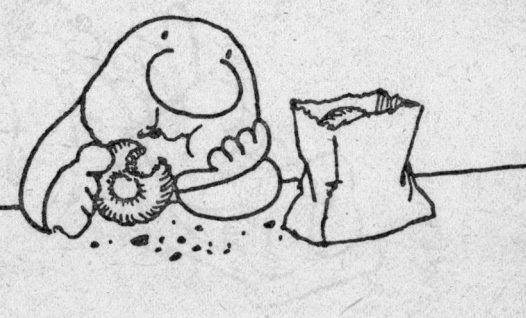

...ARE YOU TRYING TO MAKE A LIAR OUT OF ED McMAHON ?!
FUZZ
Tom Wilson

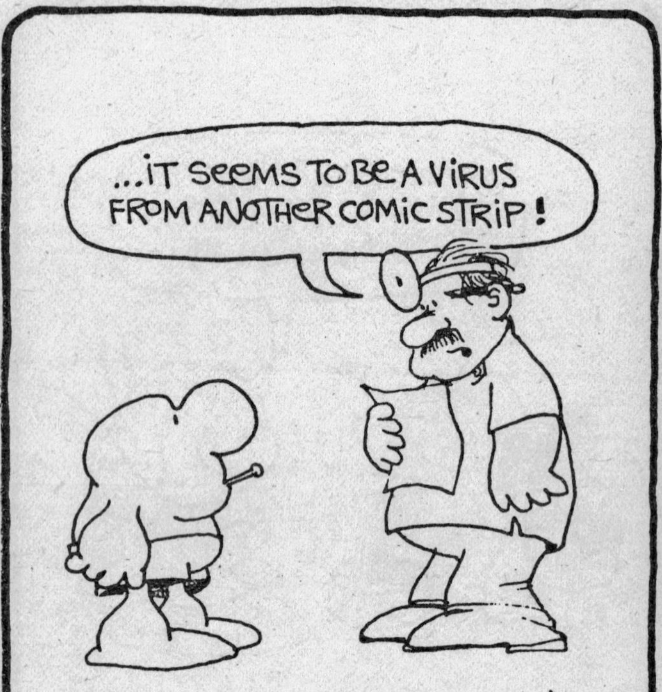
...IT SEEMS TO BE A VIRUS FROM ANOTHER COMIC STRIP!
Tom Wilson

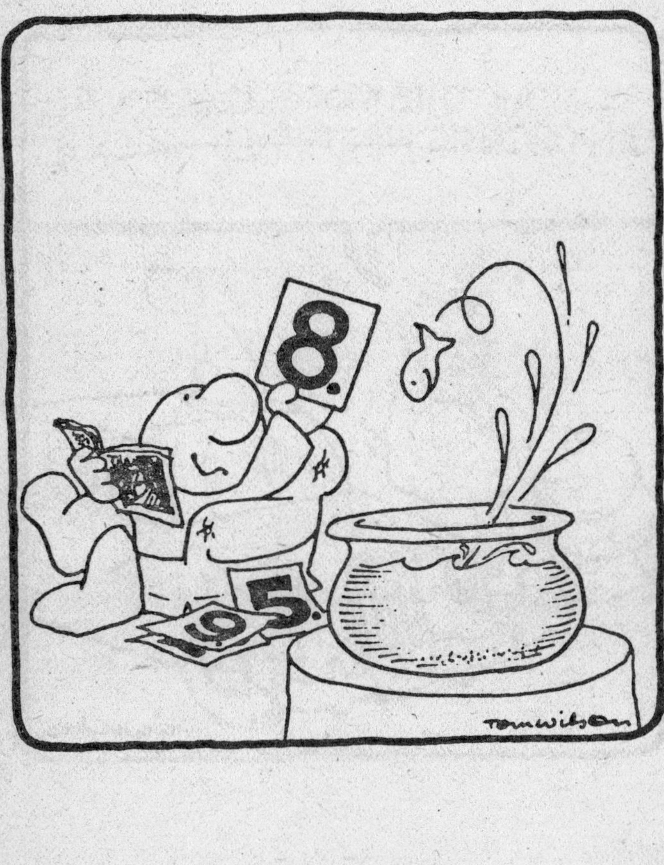
8.
5.
Tom Wilson

...NOW, THIS MODEL COMES WITH AN ORGANIC WINDSHIELD WIPER !!
TOM WILSON

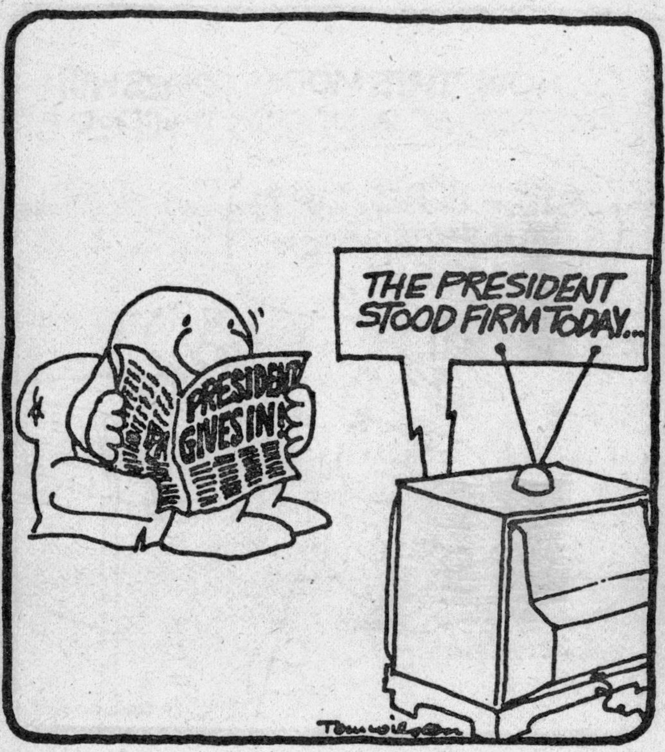
PRESIDENT GIVES IN!
THE PRESIDENT STOOD FIRM TODAY...

STIFF UPPER LIP?! ...THAT'S EASY FOR YOU TO SAY!!
BILL
OVERDUE
Tom Wilson

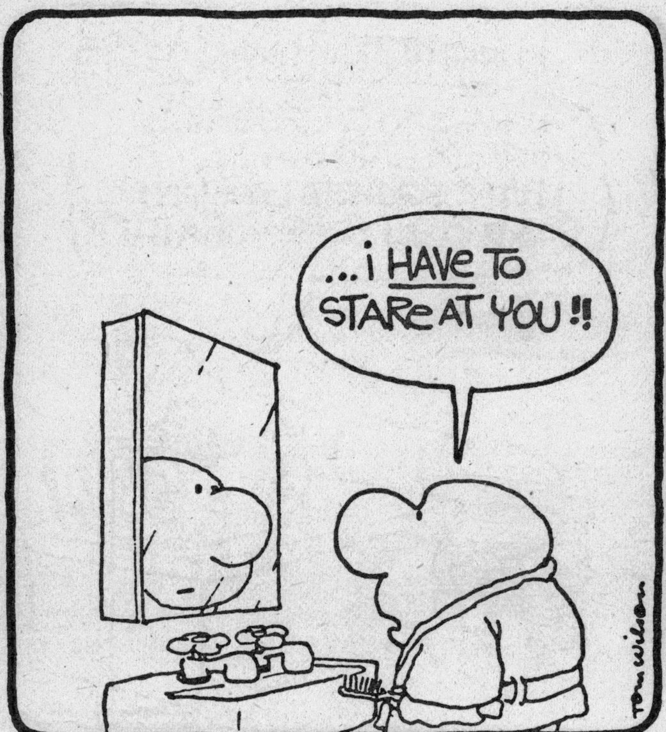
...i HAVE TO STARe AT YOU !!
tom wilson

ACE INSURANCE
WE HAVE TO CHARGE YOU HIGHER RATES... LITTLE SQUIRTS LIKE YOU TEND TO GET BEATEN UP A LOT!!
Tom Wilson

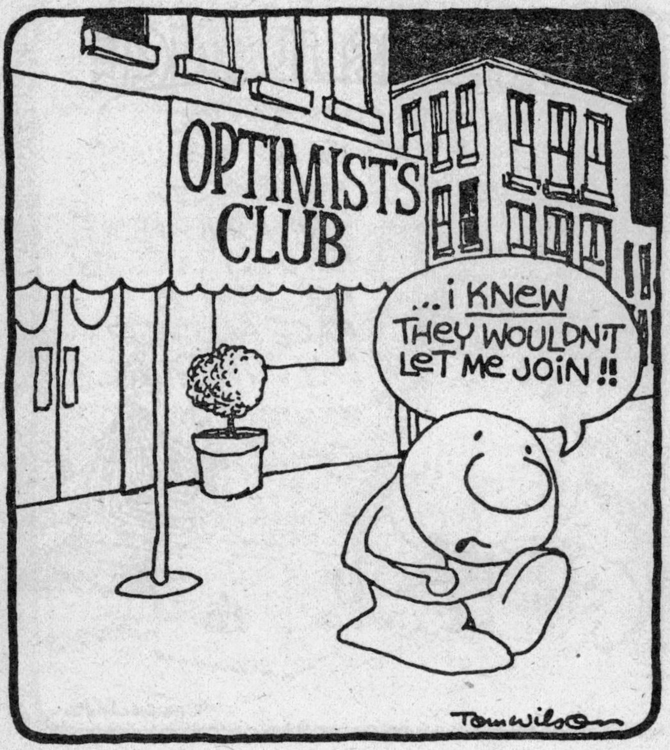
OPTIMISTS CLUB
...i KNEW THEY WOULDN'T LET ME JOIN !!
TomWilson

GOOD MORNING, MR. ZIGGY... YOUR ASSIGNMENT, IF YOU CHOOSE TO ACCEPT IT, IS TO FACE ANOTHER DAY OUT THERE!
TOM WILSON

...WHOEVER SAID BEAUTY IS ONLY SKIN DEEP ...NEVER HAD ZITS !!
TOM WILSON

ELECTRICAL SUPPLY
...NOW, CONNECT THOSE TWO LITTLE BLACK WIRES TO EACH OTHER, BUT BE CAREFUL NOT TO TOUCH THE RED WIRE.... HELLO! ..HELLO.?...

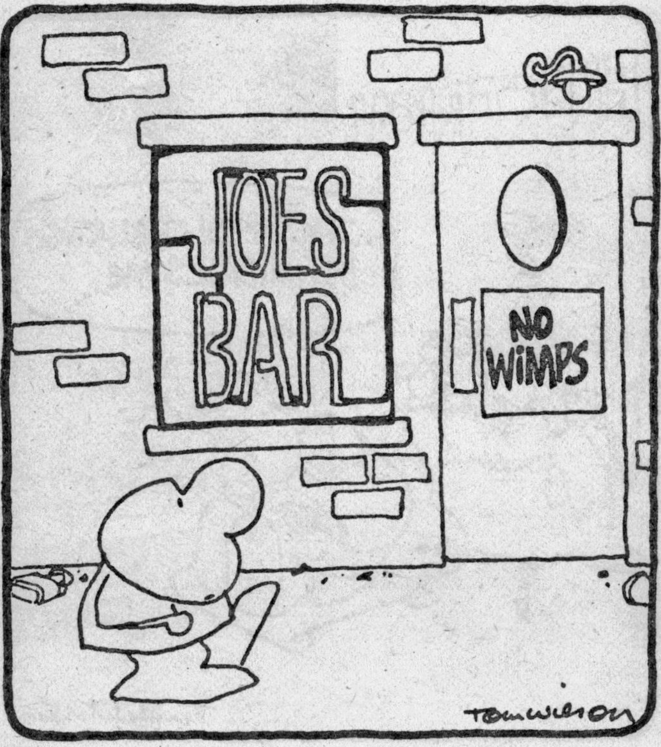
JOES
BAR
NO
WIMPS
TOM WILSON

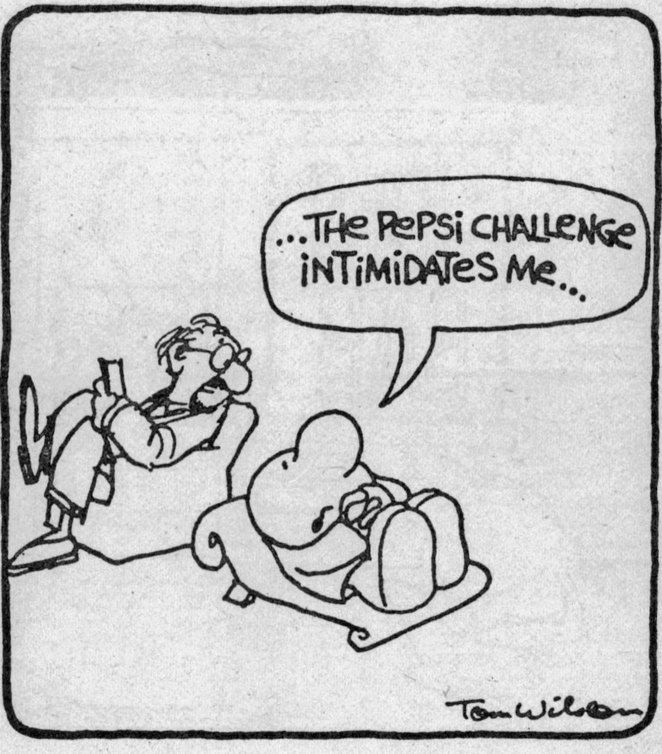
...THE PEPSI CHALLENGE INTIMIDATES ME...
Tom Wilson

...AND IN WASHINGTON TODAY TWO FEDERAL GRAND JURIES INDICTED EACH OTHER !!

FLY
UPCREEK AIRLINES
...OUR SPECIAL THIS MONTH IS THE SUPERSAVER MYSTERY BONUS...IF YOU CAN GUESS WHERE YOUR LUGGAGE WILL END UP, THE TRIP IS ON US!!
TOM WILSON

NEVER MIND STARS....
RAINDROPS MAKE ME
FEEL INSIGNIFICANT !!
Tom Wilson

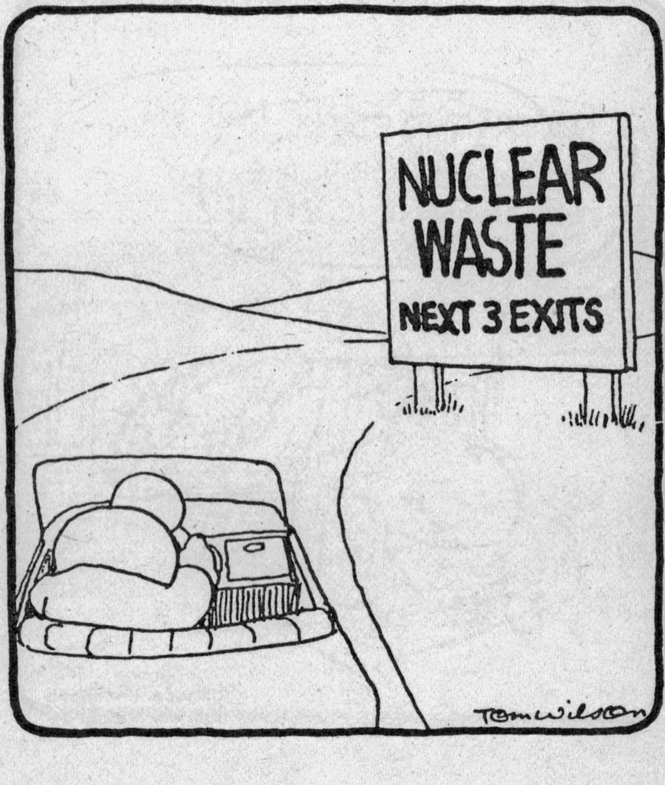
NUCLEAR
WASTE
NEXT 3 EXITS
TOM WILSON

...HOPE YOU'RE NOT IN A HURRY, SIR... MY NAILS AREN'T DRY YET!
TELLER
Tom Wilson

...THE TROUBLE WITH CURRENT EVENTS IS THAT BY THE TIME I UNDERSTAND WHAT THEY ARE... ...THEY AREN'T !!
Tom Wilson

...NEVER MIND THE CRACKER, ..I'LL JUST HAVE WHAT YOU'RE HAVING !!
CRACKER
TOM WILSON

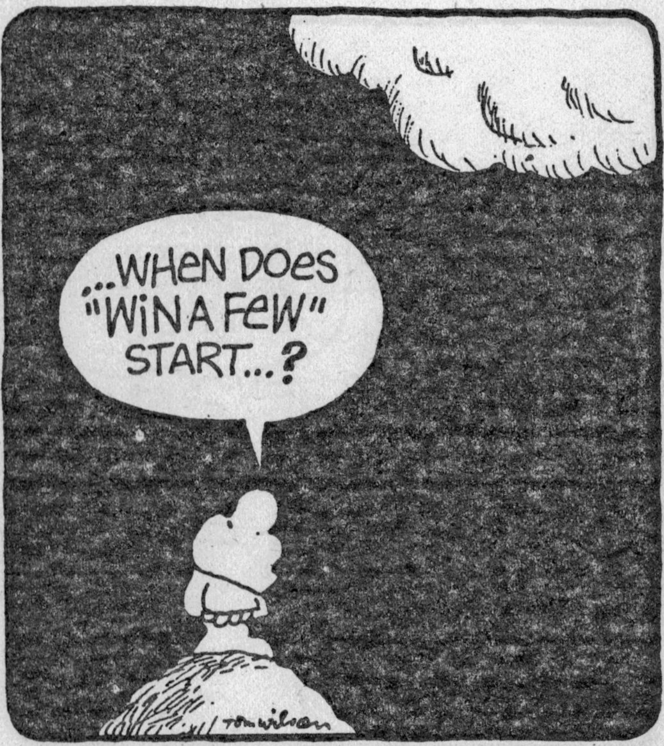
...WHEN DOES "WIN A FEW" START...?
Tom Wilson

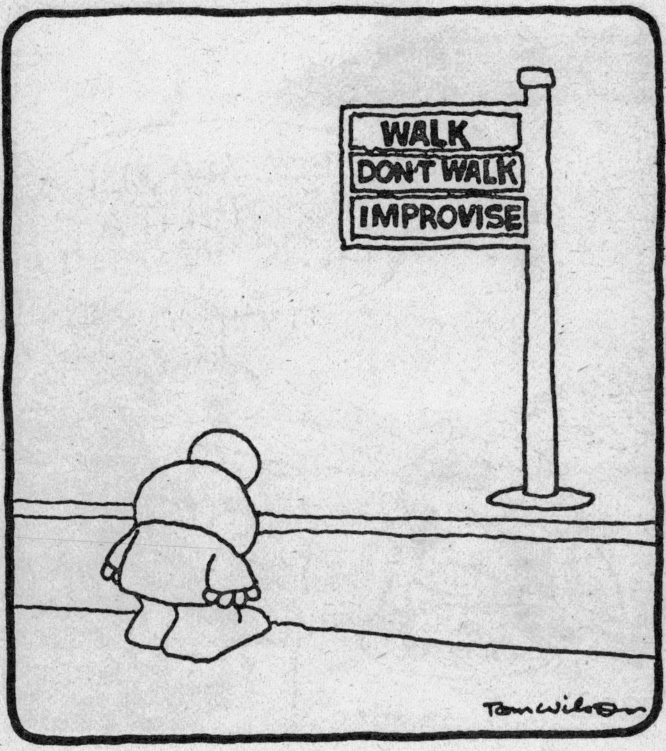
WALK
DON'T WALK
IMPROVISE
Tom Wilson

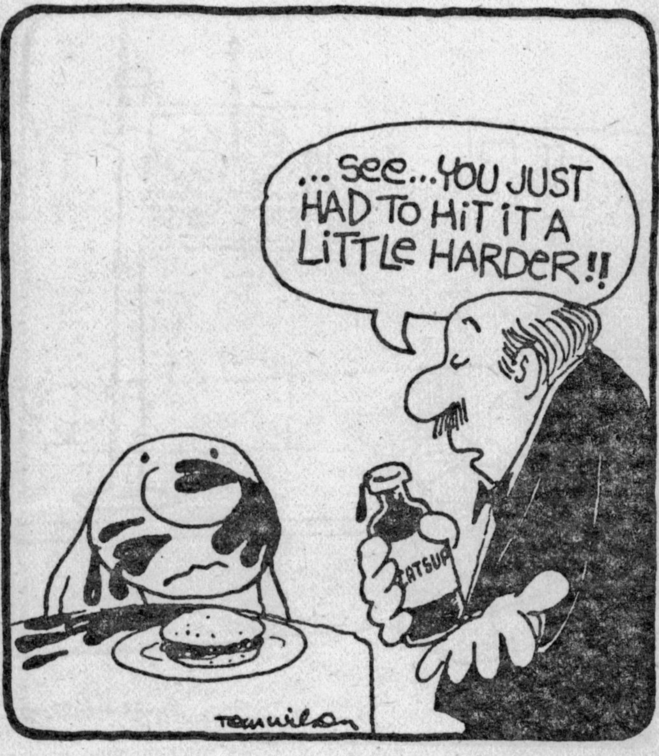
...SEE...YOU JUST HAD TO HIT IT A LITTLE HARDER!!
KATSUP
tom wilson

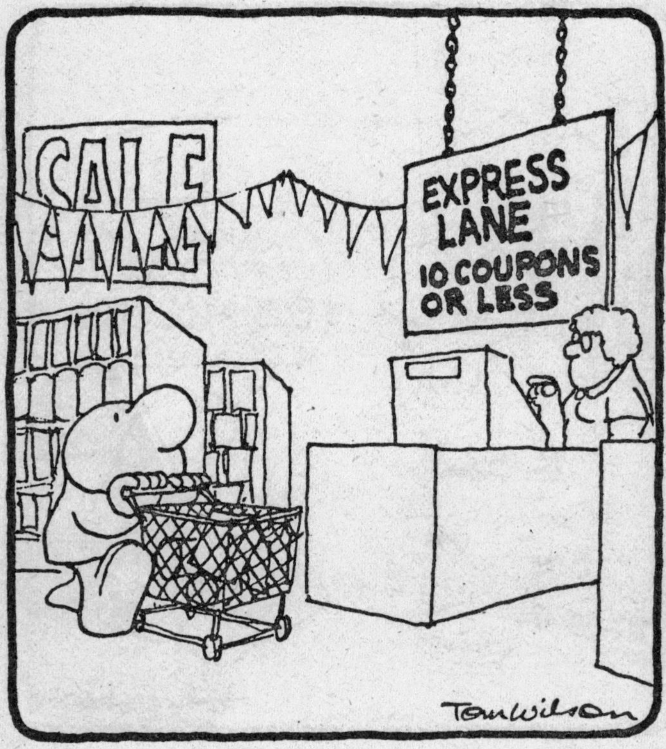
SALE
EXPRESS LANE
10 COUPONS OR LESS
Tom Wilson

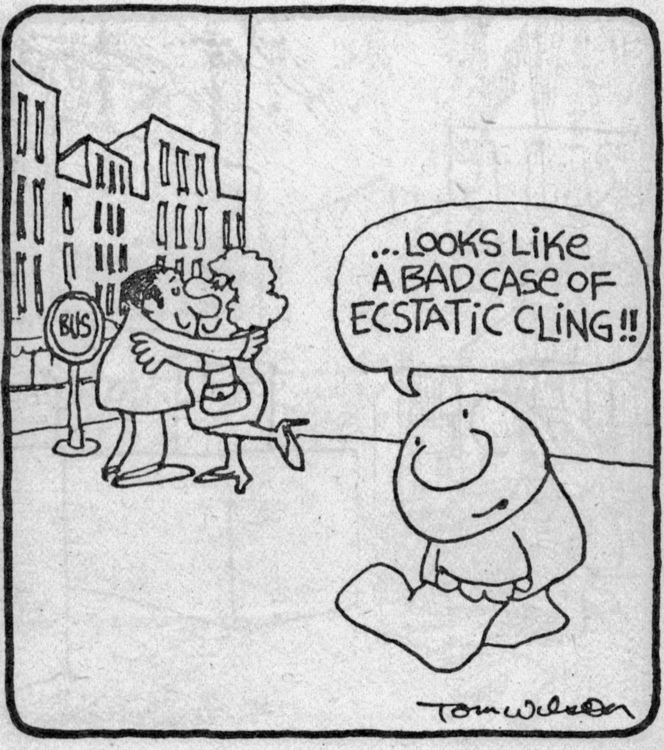
BUS
...LOOKS LIKE A BAD CASE OF ECSTATIC CLING!!
Tom Wilson

WOULD SOMEBODY PLEASE TELL THE EDITOR THAT THEY'VE GOT ME IN THE WRONG COMIC STRIP TODAY ?!!..
Tom Wilson

SOLITUDE CAN BE A VERY INTROSPECTIVE EXPERIENCE ...IT GIVES YOU AN OPPORTUNITY TO REEVALUATE YOUR PRIORITIES, BEING ALONE CAUSES YOU TO GET A BETTER FOCUS ON WHO YOU ARE, ..AND MOST OF ALL IT HELPS YOU TO BETTER APPRECIATE NOT BEING ALONE...
Tom Wilson

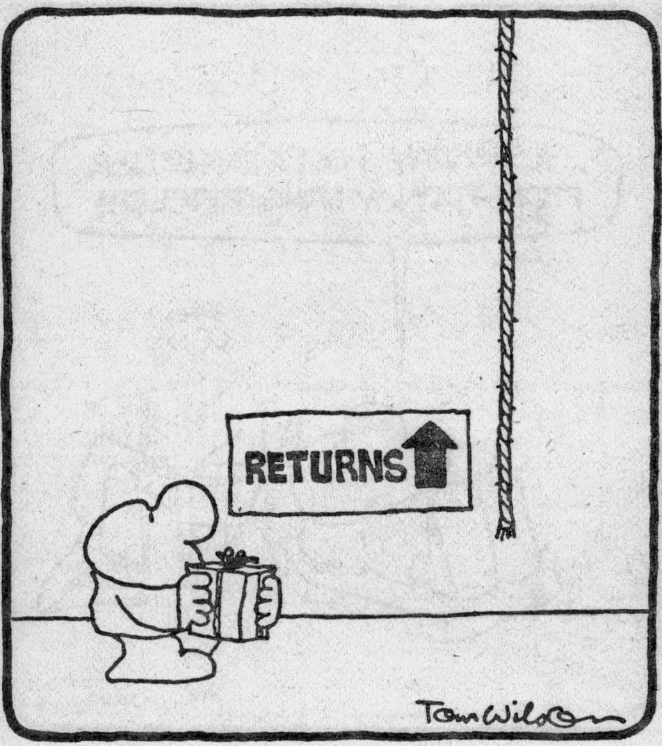
RETURNS
Tom Wilson

...YESTERDAY I GOT A FAN LETTER FROM RODNEY DANGERFIELD!!
Tom Wilson

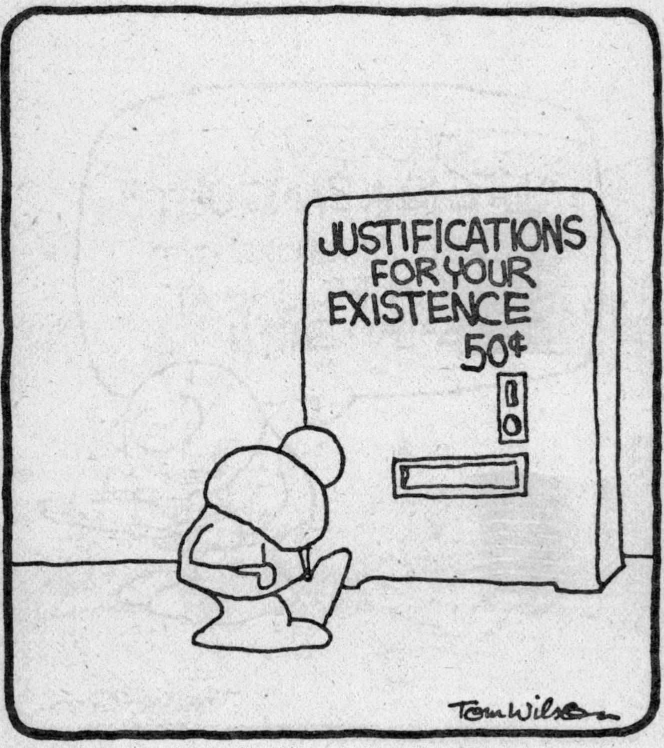
JUSTIFICATIONS FOR YOUR EXISTENCE
50¢
Tom Wilson

THEY SAY "LIFE IS A BANQUET" ...BUT SOMEHOW I GOT STUCK IN THE LINE AT THE SALAD BAR !!
Tom Wilson

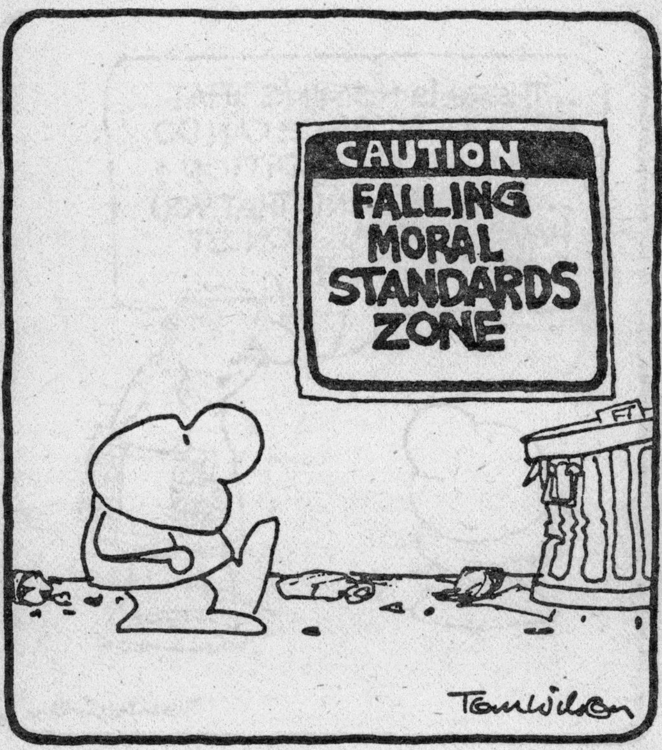
CAUTION
FALLING MORAL STANDARDS ZONE
TomWilson

...THERE IS NOTHING THAT MEDICAL SCIENCE CAN DO ABOUT YOUR CONDITION! ...I RECOMMEND THAT YOU HAVE YOUR CARTOONIST REDRAW YOU!!
Tom Wilson

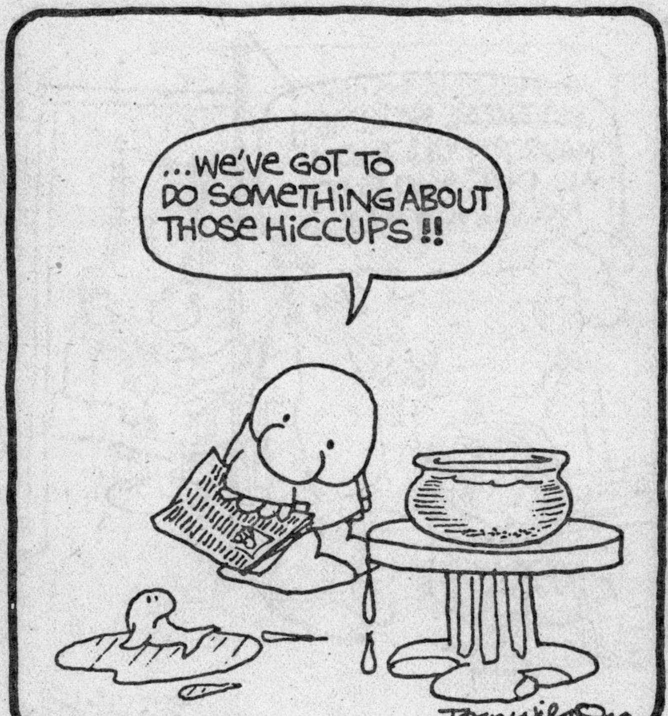
...WE'VE GOT TO DO SOMETHING ABOUT THOSE HICCUPS !!
Tom Wilson

...i GUESS WE'LL JUST HAVE TO PULL THEM ALL OUT, AND PUT NEW ONES iN !!
RECEPTIONIST
Tom Wilson

...NO OFFENSE, BUT I'D RATHER SPEAK DIRECTLY TO MR. KARL MALDEN, PLEASE!
AMERICAN EXPRESS
Tom Wilson

SORRY....NO GAG TODAY ...THE CARTOON CHARACTER WHO WAS SUPPOSED TO PLAY THE MUGGER IN TODAY'S CARTOON GOT MUGGED ON THE WAY OVER HERE !!
HOTEL
TOM WILSON

...ONE THING ABOUT UNEMPLOYMENT... THERE'S A NICE BIG AUDIENCE FOR THE LABOR DAY PARADE!!
Tom Wilson

...THERE'S NO VALID PSYCHOLOGICAL REASON FOR YOU TO HAVE A GUILT COMPLEX ... YOU HAVE NO ONE BUT YOURSELF TO BLAME !!
Tom Wilson

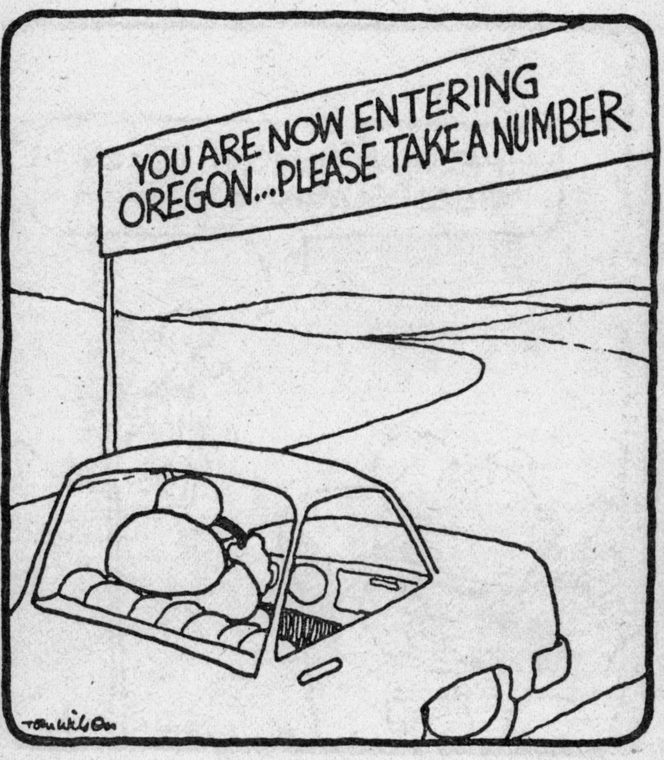
YOU ARE NOW ENTERING
OREGON...PLEASE TAKE A NUMBER

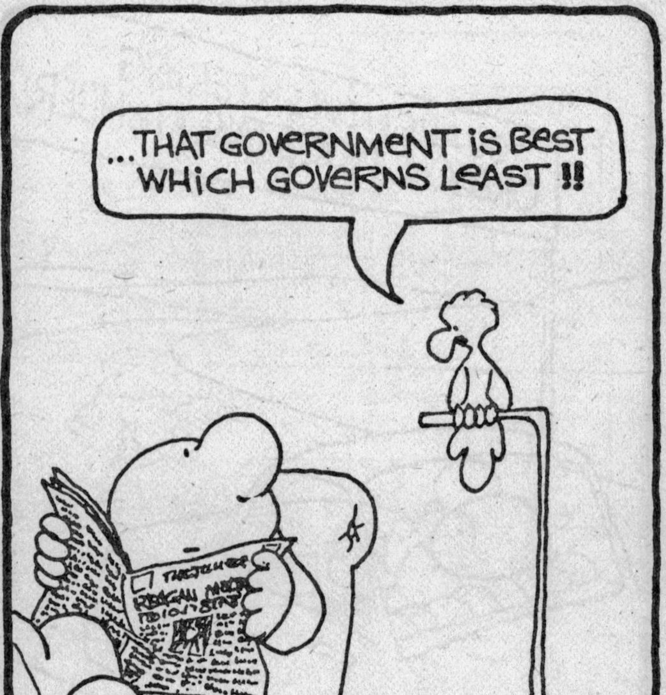
...THAT GOVERNMENT IS BEST WHICH GOVERNS LEAST !!
Tom Wilson

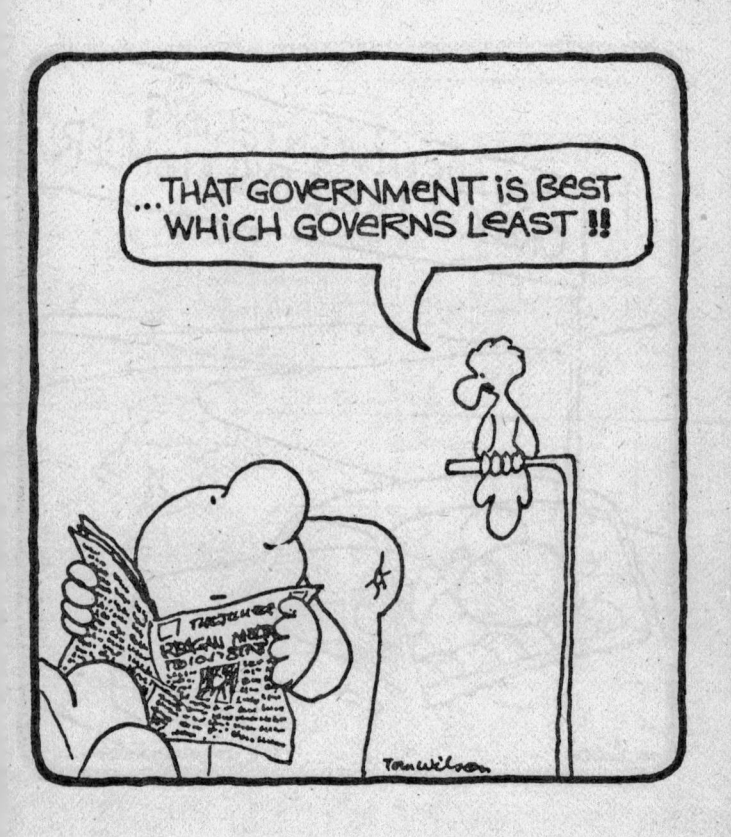

DENTIST
HAPPY HOUR 3 P.M. TO 4:30 P.M.
...HE USES LAUGHING GAS!
RECEPTIONIST
Tom Wilson

...YOU DON'T SEEM TO HAVE DECLARED THE QUARTER YOU FOUND IN A VENDING MACHINE LAST OCTOBER THIRD...
I.R.S.
TOM WILSON

...BEATS ME... I HAVEN'T HAD A POLITICAL OPINION SINCE DOONESBURY LEFT THE NEWSPAPER !!
POLIT-I-POLL
Tom Wilson

...I'M JUST CURIOUS... EXACTLY HOW CAN A BOTTLE OF DISTILLED WATER BE "NEW AND IMPROVED"?
Distilled WATER

...FOR THOSE OF YOU WHO JUST JOINED US... LET'S BE A LITTLE MORE PROMPT OUT THERE IN THE FUTURE!! OKAY?!
Tom Wilson

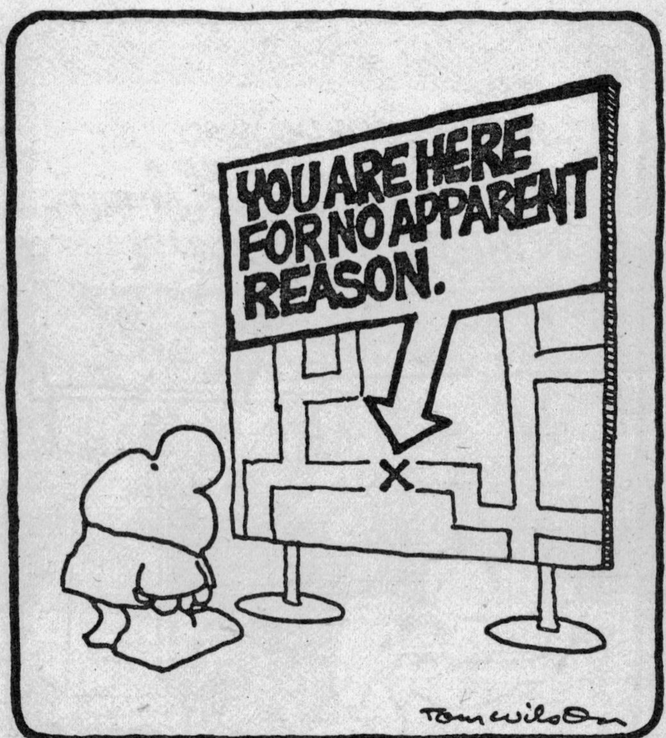
YOU ARE HERE
FOR NO APPARENT
REASON.
X
Tom Wilson

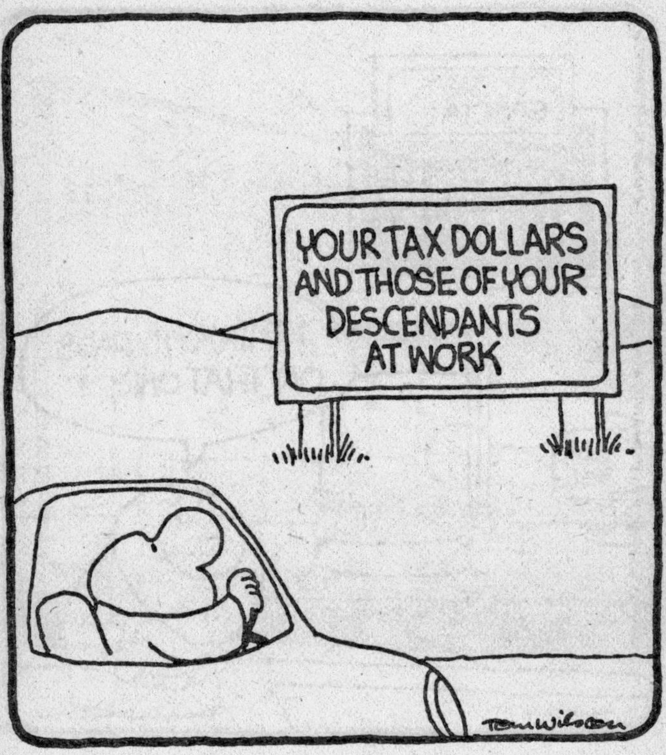
YOUR TAX DOLLARS AND THOSE OF YOUR DESCENDANTS AT WORK

TODAY'S SPECIAL
TIME-RELEASE CHILI $1.25
...I THINK I'LL PASS ON THAT ONE!

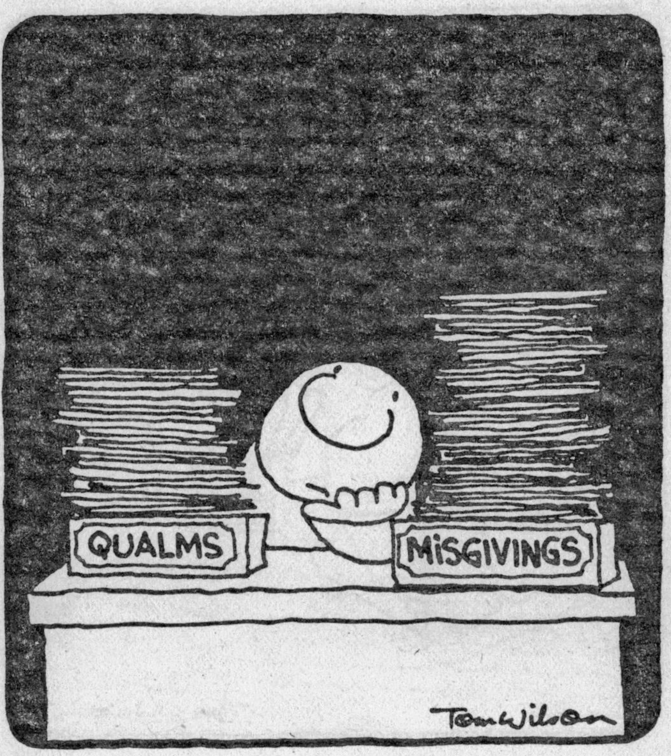
QUALMS
MiSGIVINGS
Tom Wilson

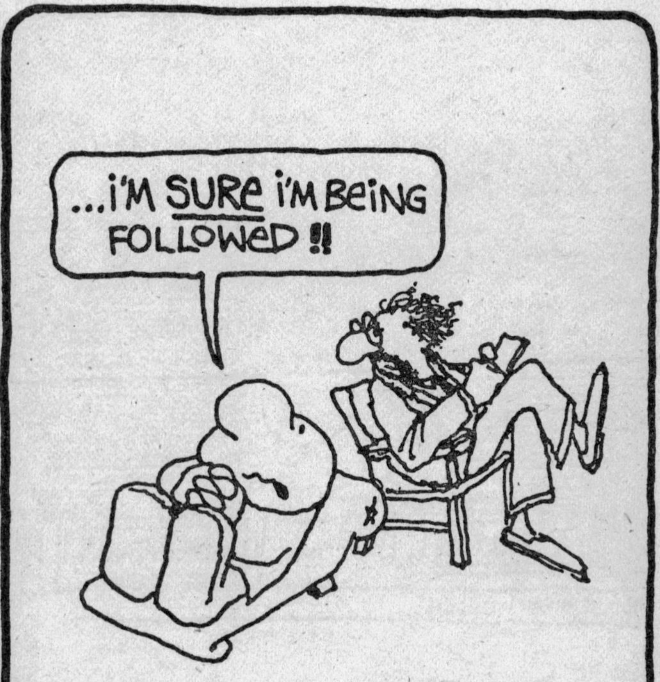
...i'M SURE i'M BEING FOLLOWED !!
Tom Wilson

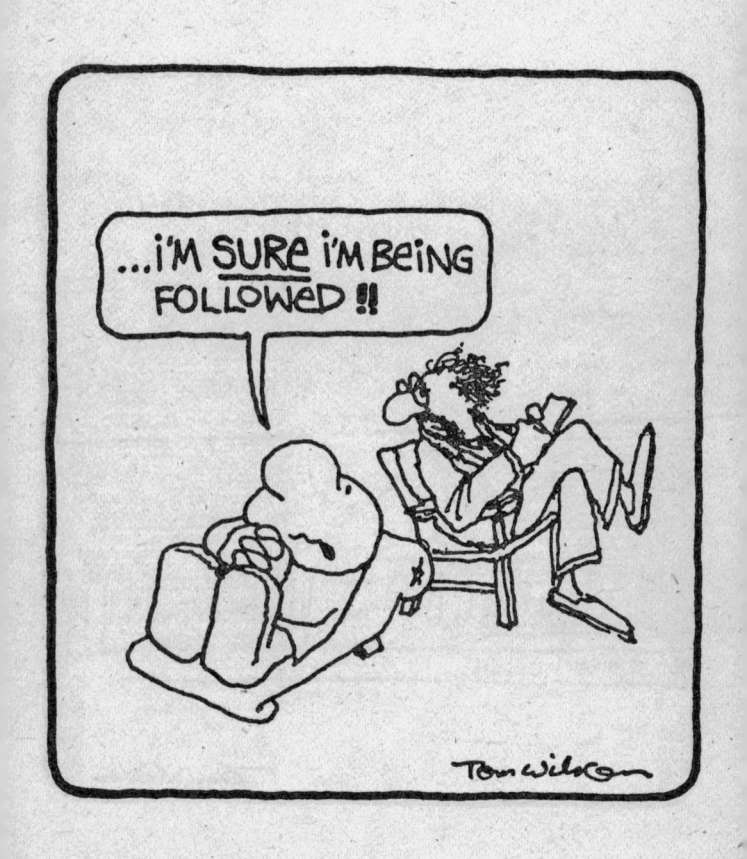

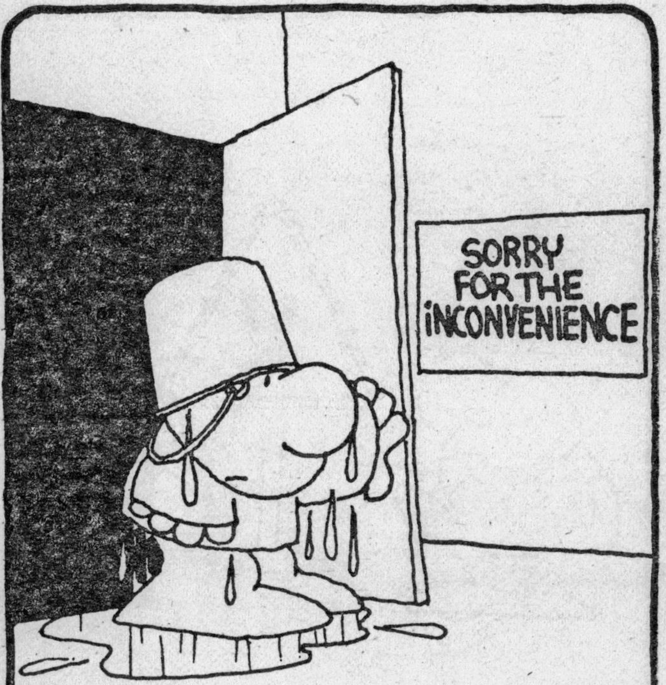
SORRY FOR THE INCONVENIENCE
Tom Wilson

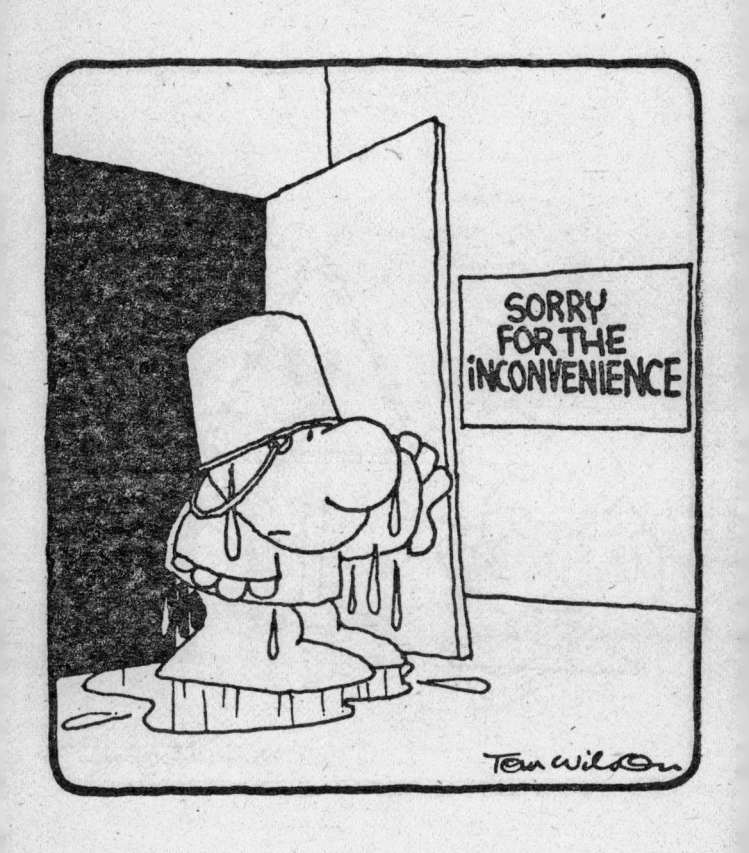

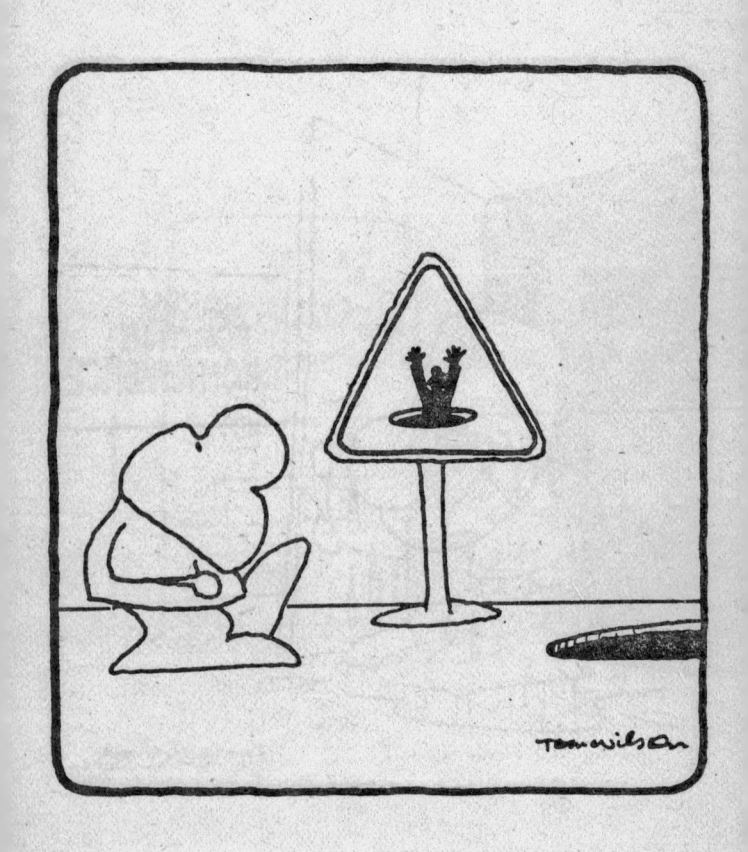

LEGAL
RECOURSE
50¢
Tom Wilson

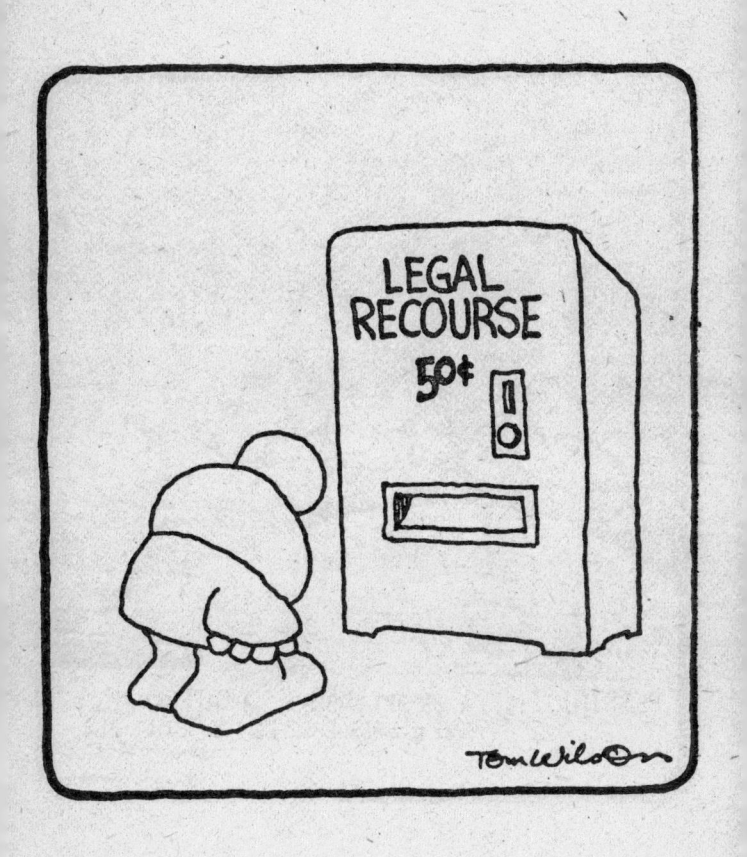

PESSIMIST: A person who sees a falling star, and wishes that it won't hit him.

...MY iDEA OF A GREAT SEVEN-COURSE MEAL IS SIX OREOS AND A GLASS OF MILK !!
Tom Wilson

PERSONAL COMPUTERS
I'D LIKE TO RETURN THIS .. IT GETS TOO PERSONAL!
Tom Wilson

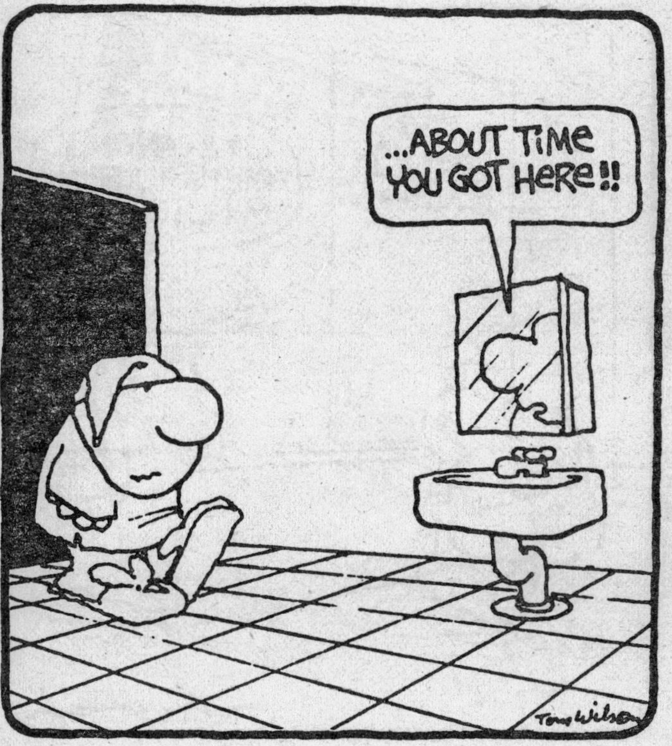
...ABOUT TIME YOU GOT HERE!!
Tom Wilson

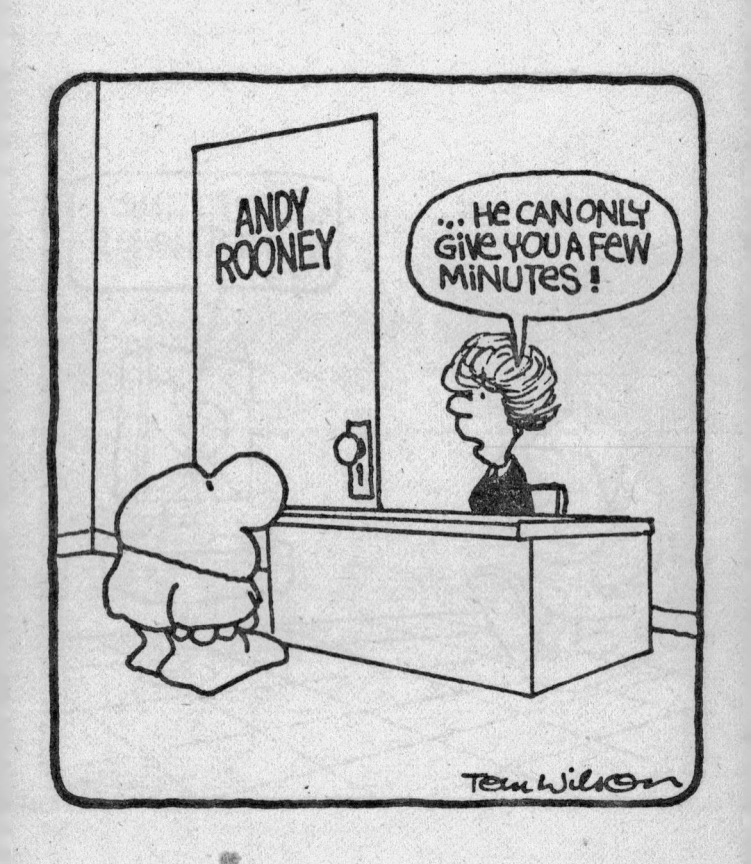
ANDY ROONEY
... HE CAN ONLY GIVE YOU A FEW MINUTES!
Tom Wilson

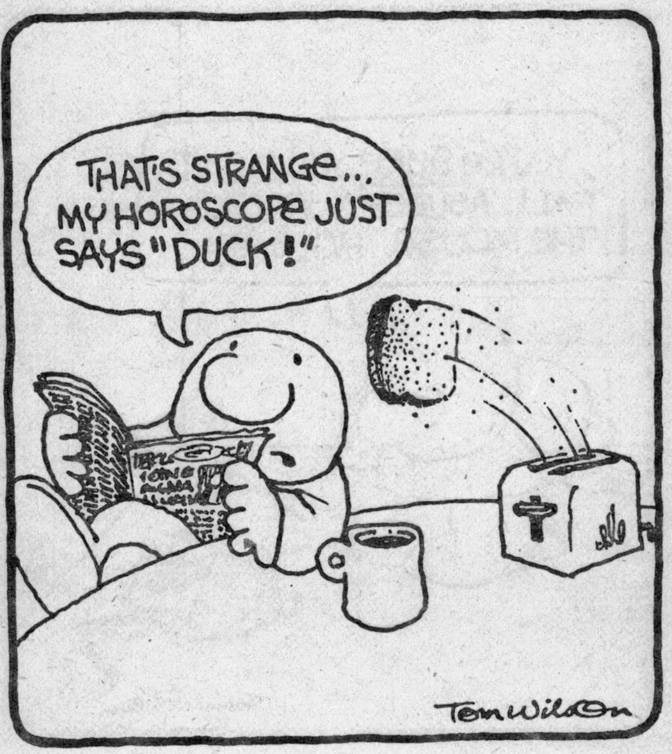
THAT'S STRANGE...
MY HOROSCOPE JUST
SAYS "DUCK!"
Tom Wilson

...YOU'RE SURE YOU DIDN'T FALL ASLEEP GUARDING THE MOUSE HOLE ?!
KICK ME
Tom Wilson

...ER...UH... I DON'T SUPPOSE YOU'D LIKE TO ENROLL IN AN ASSERTIVENESS TRAINING CLASS ...WOULD YOU ?
Tom Wilson

DOC, I'VE DECIDED TO BECOME MORE ASSERTIVE! ...I MEAN, PROVIDING OF COURSE THAT'S O.K. WITH YOU ....
Tom Wilson

ASSERTIVENESS TRAINING CLASS
...NOW, FIRST OFF, I WANT EACH OF YOU TO TURN TO YOUR NEIGHBOR AND GIVE HIM A LITTLE SHOVE!

ASSERTIVENESS TRAINING CLASS
ALL RIGHT, CLASS. THAT CONCLUDES OUR COURSE !! ...NOW I WANT YOU TO GET OUT THERE WITH THE ATTITUDE THAT YOU'RE TOP DOG ...AND EVERYONE ELSE IS A FIRE HYDRANT !!!
TOM WILSON

ASSERT YOURSELF!
OH YEAH !! ...WELL JUST REMEMBER, WISE GUY... WITHOUT ME, YOU'D BE NOTHING !!!
TOM WILSON

REMEMBER... ASSERT YOURSELF !!
...ER...UH... MAKE THAT TWO SCOOPS !!
TOM WILSON

PLEASE STAND BY... WE HAVE TEMPORARILY LOST OUR CANNED LAUGHTER...

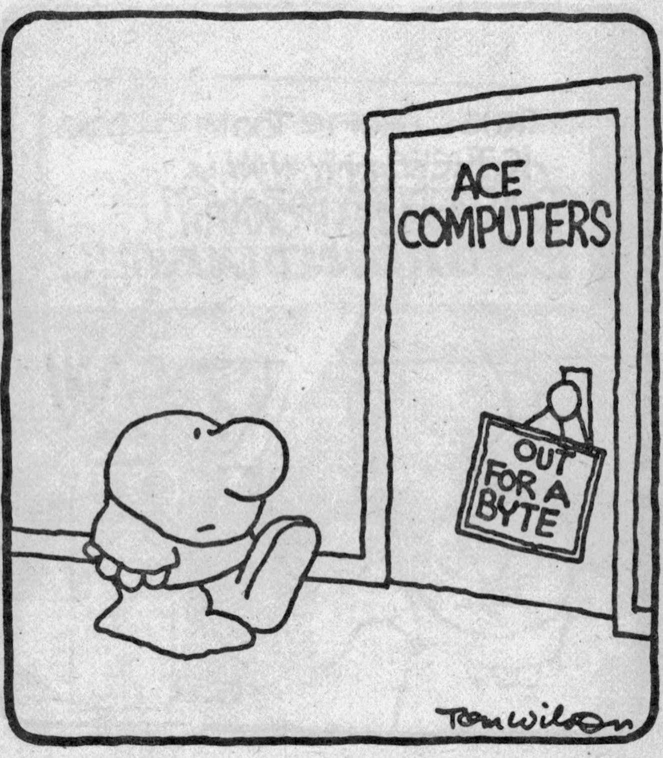
ACE
COMPUTERS
OUT
FOR A
BYTE
Tom Wilson

I TRUST PEOPLE TOO MUCH, DOC ...IS THERE ANY WAY YOU COULD INDUCE PARANOIA?!
Tom Wilson

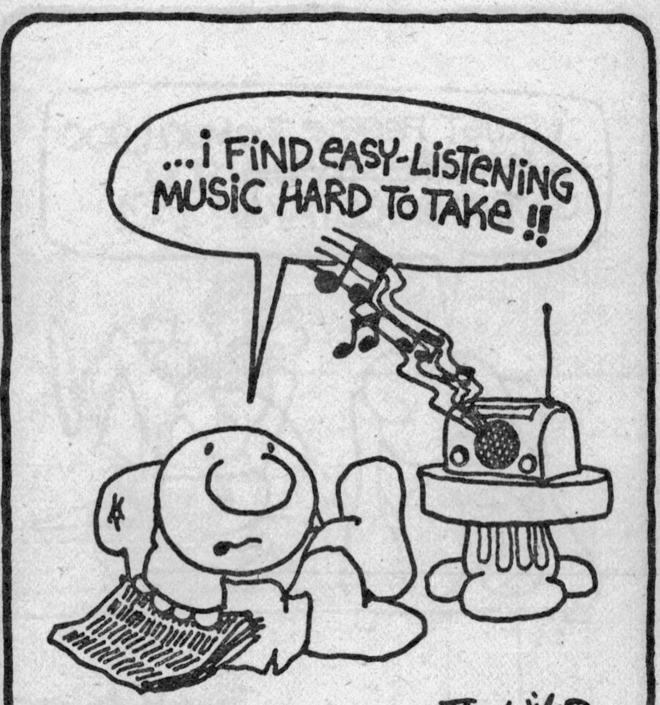
...i FIND EASY-LISTENING MUSIC HARD TO TAKE !!
Tom Wilson

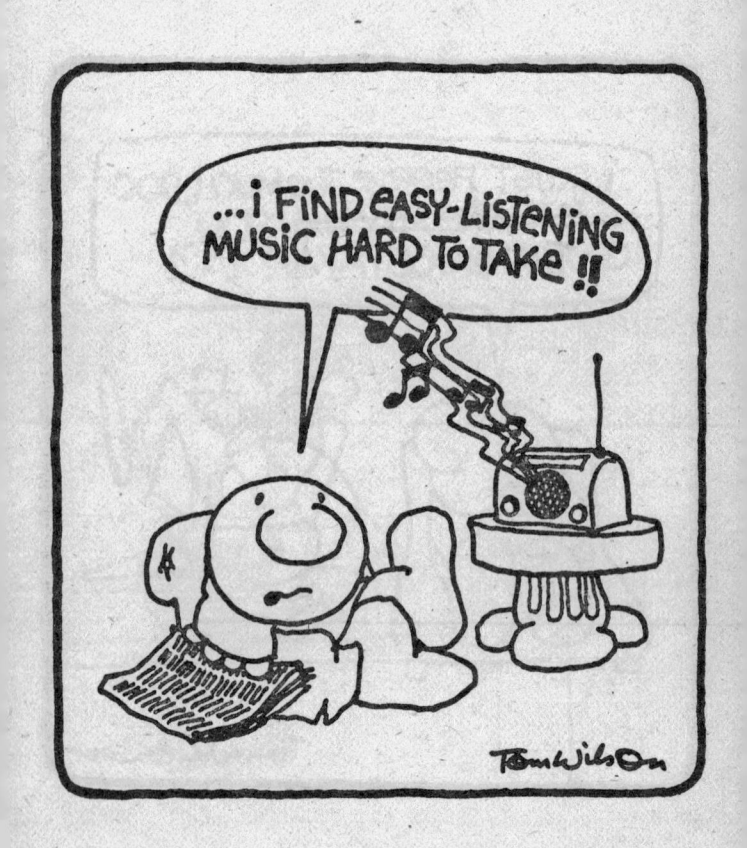

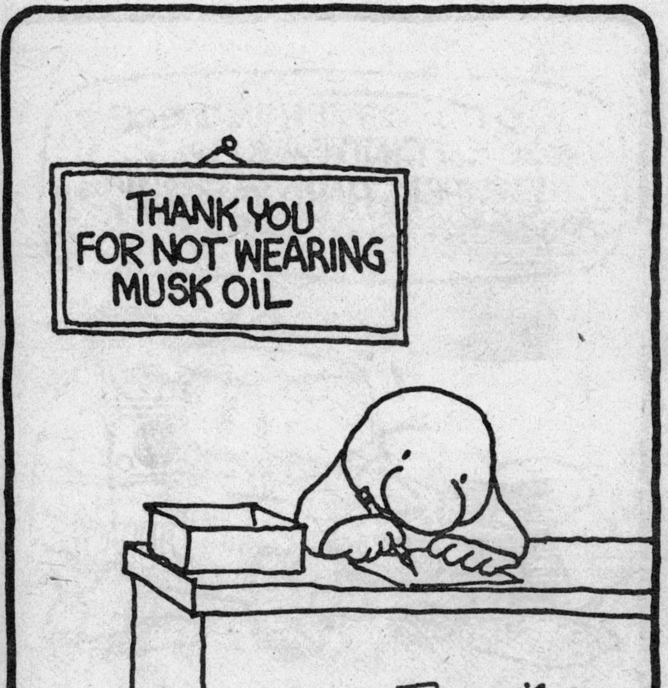
THANK YOU
FOR NOT WEARING
MUSK OIL
Tom Wilson

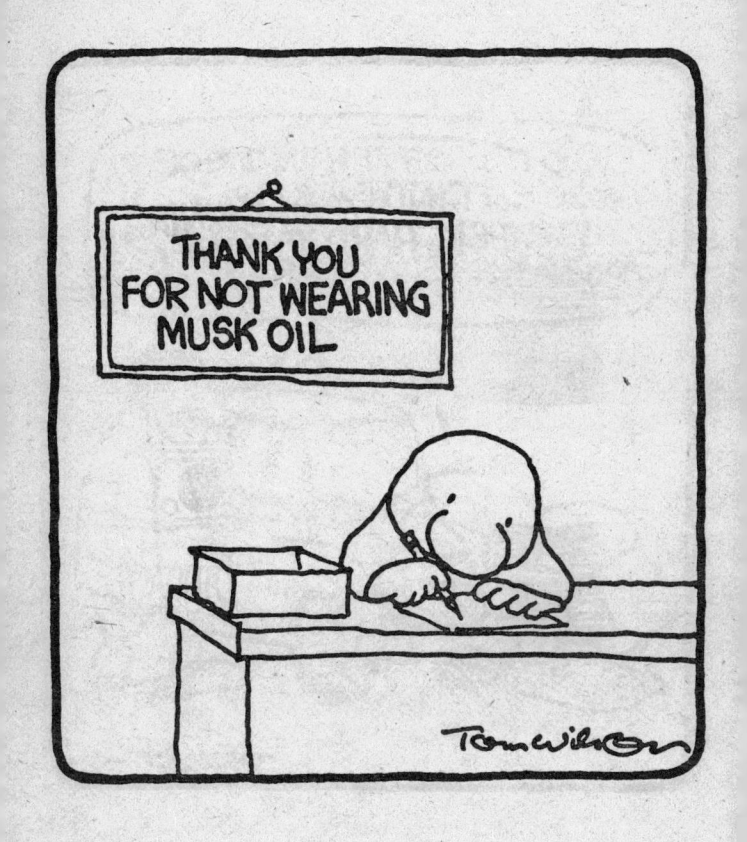

...AND IT DOESN'T HAVE ONE OF THOSE EXPENSIVE AIR BAGS... JUST THIS LIGHT THAT COMES ON AND SAYS "SAYONARA!"
Tom Wilson

SALE
T.V. DINNERS
LIMITED WARRANTY
THINGS
CORNED
LO-CAL
PIZZA
AND RICE
TomWilson

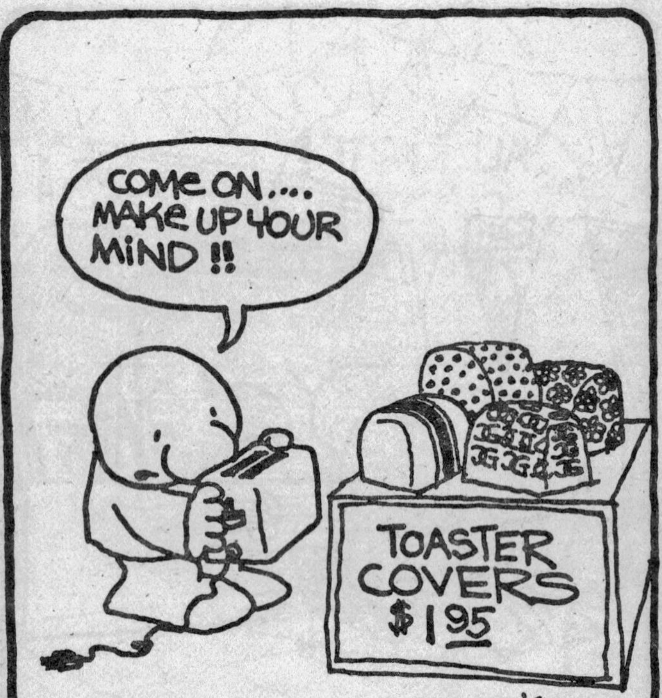
COME ON....
MAKE UP YOUR
MIND !!
TOASTER
COVERS
$1 95
Tom Wilson

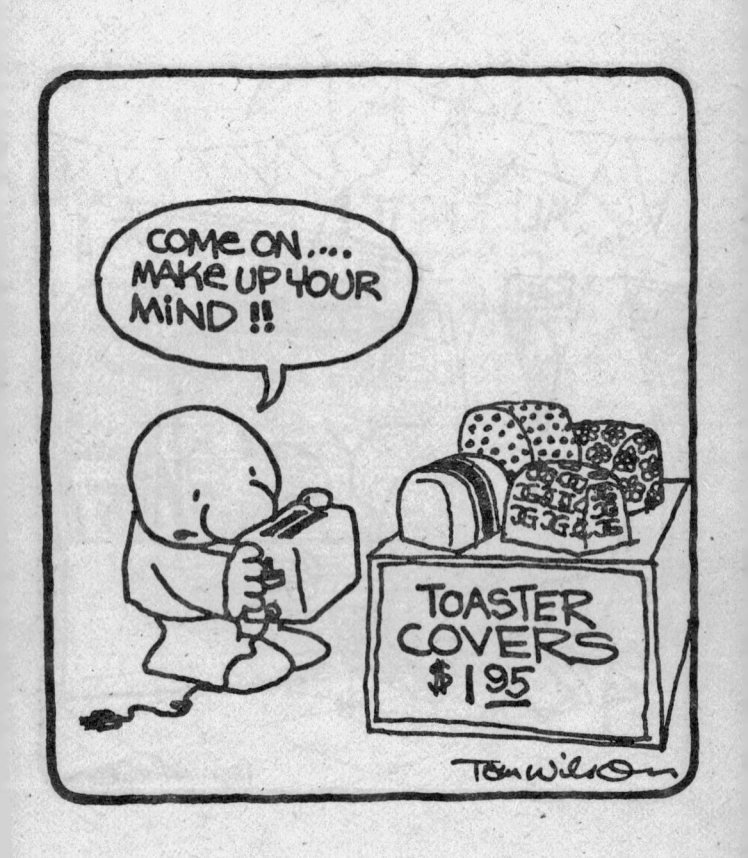

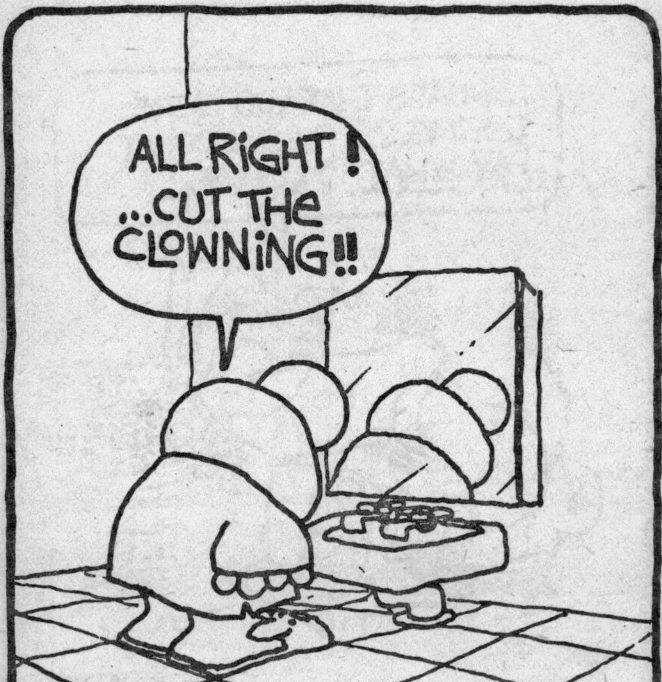
ALL RIGHT! ...CUT THE CLOWNING!!

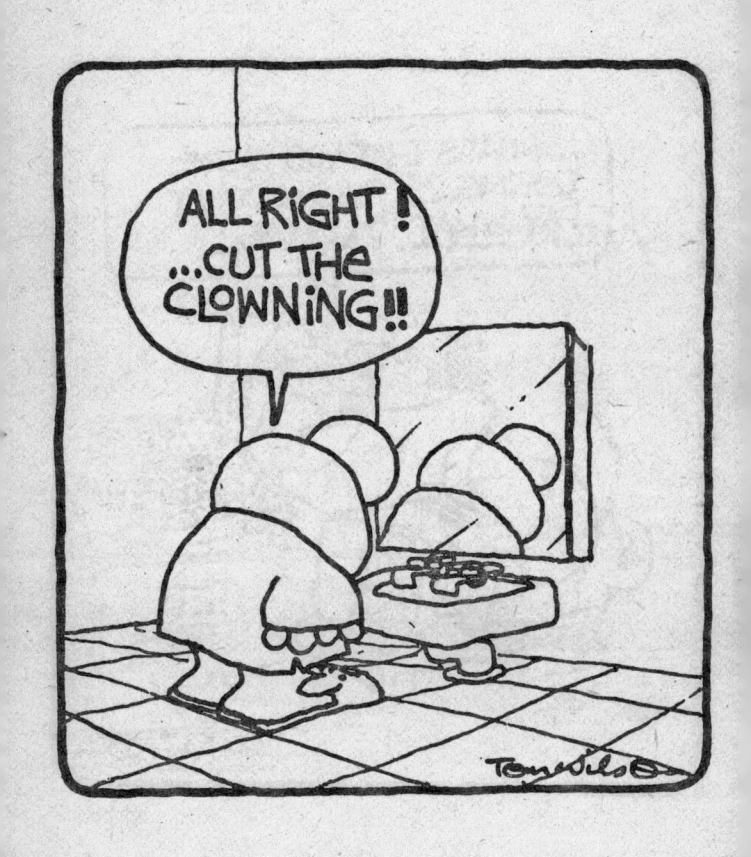

...WHAT'S THAT YOU WERE SAYING ?... PEOPLE DON'T PAY WHAT TO YOU ?...
Tom Wilson

YES, IT WAS TEN DOLLARS FOR THE DOCTOR TO SEE YOU ..BUT HE ALSO TALKED TO YOU!!
BILL
Tom Wilson

...i THINK MY CAREER PROBLEM IS THAT i DON'T HAVE ANY RANK TO PULL !!
Tom Wilson

TV ISN'T TRUE TO LIFE
....BUT THEN, SOMETIMES NEITHER IS LIFE !!
Tom Wilson

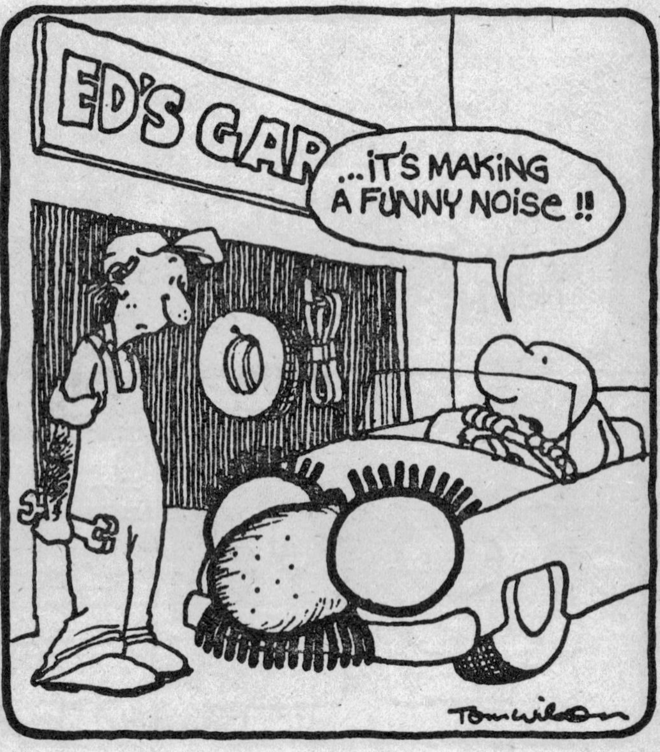
ED'S GAR
...IT'S MAKING A FUNNY NOISE !!
Tom Wilson

IF NOT COMPLETELY SATISFIED... WHO iS THESE DAYS !!
MENU
TOM WILSON

I'M SORRY, SIR...
BUT WE CAN'T CASH CHECKS
FOR NO-ACCOUNT PEOPLE !!
TELLER
TOM WILSON

POST OFFICE
...IF YOU'RE SENDING IT FOURTH CLASS, SIR, WE'D LIKE YOU TO ADD THE ADDRESSEE'S NEXT OF KIN !!
Tom Wilson

PORTIONS OF THE FOLLOWING PROGRAM MAY BE OFFENSIVE TO COMIC-STRIP CHARACTERS...
Tom Wilson

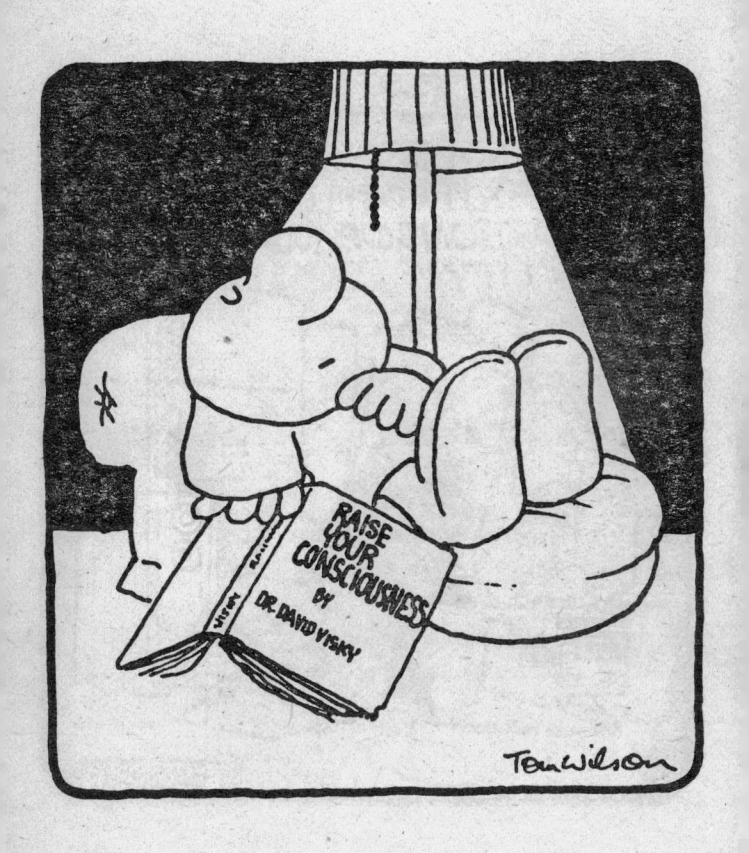
RAISE
YOUR
CONSCIOUSNESS
BY
DR. DAVID VISKY
Tom Wilson

...IT'S NOT BROKEN, BUT COULD YOU FIX IT SO IT'LL GIVE ME A MILD ELECTRIC SHOCK WHEN I OPEN IT?
MR. FIXIT
Tom Wilson

INFORMATION
...WILL DEAN MARTIN AND JERRY LEWIS EVER GET BACK TOGETHER AGAIN?
Tom Wilson

...SOME GUY HERE CLAIMS TO RUN HIS CAR ON CHICKEN MANURE •...WHAT DO YOU THINK OF THAT?
Tom Wilson

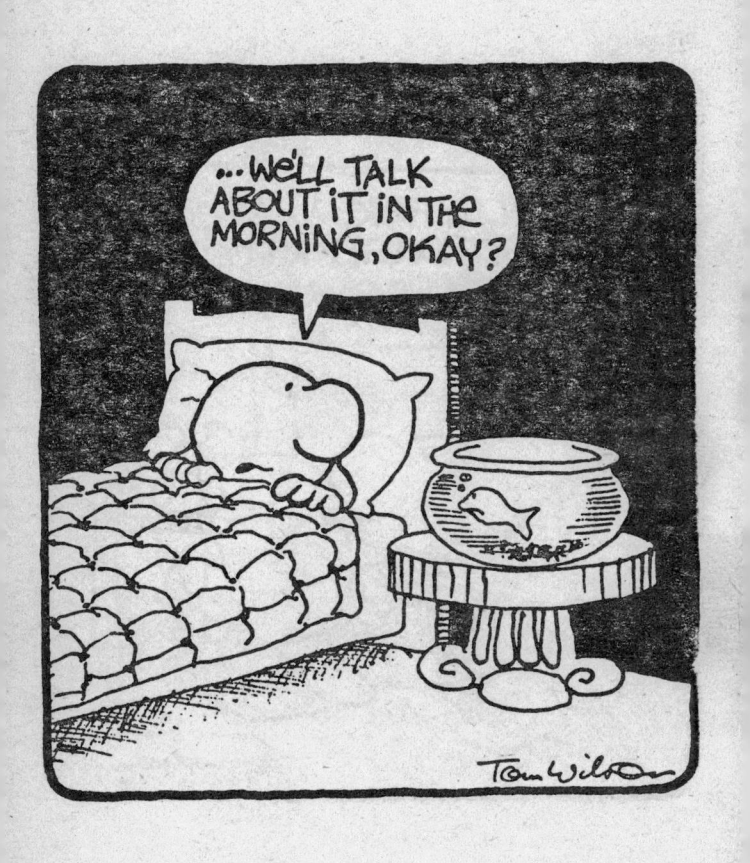
...WE'LL TALK ABOUT IT IN THE MORNING, OKAY?
Tom Wilson

...NOW, BEHAVE YOURSELF, OR I'LL TRANSFER YOU TO A CAT COMIC STRIP !!
TOM WILSON